THE UNTAMED WORLD

Lions

Jonathan Bocknek

RAINTREE
STECK-VAUGHN
PUBLISHERS

A Harcourt Company

Austin   New York
www.raintreesteckvaughn.com

Published by Raintree Steck-Vaughn Publishers, an imprint of Steck-Vaughn Company.

Library of Congress Cataloging-in-Publication Data

Bocknek, Jonathan.
    Lions/Jonathan Bocknek.
    p. cm. -- (Untamed world)
    Includes bibliographical references (p.).
    ISBN 0-8172-4577-4
    1. Lions--Juvenile literature. [1. Lions.] I. Title. II. Series.

    QL737.C23 B64 2001
    599.757--dc21

                                                   2001019200

Printed and bound in Canada
1234567890 05 04 03 02 01

Project Editor
Leslie Strudwick

Design and Illustration
Warren Clark

Project Coordinator
Heather Kissock

Raintree Steck-Vaughn Editor
Pam Wells

Copy Editors
Krista McLuskey
Janice Parker

Consultants
David Cumming has been involved in wildlife conservation and research in Zimbabwe for more than thirty years. He is Senior Conservation Advisor with World Wildlife Fund's Southern Africa Regional Program.

Acknowledgments
The publisher wishes to thank Warren Rylands for inspiring this series.

Photograph Credits
Canada In Stock/Ivy Images: pages 24, 39 (Michael Fairchild); **Corel Corporation:** cover, pages 7, 12 bottom, 17, 21, 27, 31, 59, 60, 61; **Steve Hoffman:** page 57; **Ivy Images:** page 13 (Philip van den Berg); **Brian Keating:** pages 12 top, 14, 18, 26, 30, 35, 55; **Samantha McCrory:** page 45; **Krista McLuskey:** page 5; **Tom Myers:** page 54; **Photofest:** pages 9, 53; **Tom Stack and Associates:** pages 4 (Thomas Kitchin), 22 (John Shaw); **J.D. Taylor:** pages 6, 11, 16, 19, 23, 28, 29, 37, 38, 40, 41, 52; **Visuals Unlimited:** pages 15 (Walt Anderson), 20 (Fritz Pölking), 25 (Gerald & Buff Corsi), 32 (Will Troyer), 34 (Joe McDonald); **E. Melanie Watt:** pages 42, 43.

Contents

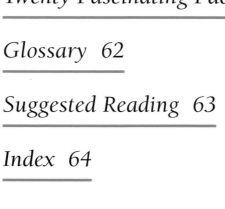

Features

Lions are one of the ...'s most feared and deadly ... predators.

Opposite: A lion's roar can be heard for miles.

Lions are the second-largest cats in the world. Only tigers are bigger.

Lions share much in common with the pet cat you have at home or see in your neighborhood: sharp, curved claws; a tight, muscular body; powerful legs and paws; and excellent eyesight and hearing. However, lions are not good pets nor are they the cute, cuddly animals often shown in cartoons. They are one of the planet's most feared and deadly predators.

Male lions are much larger and stronger than females. What they gain in strength, though, they lose in agility. They are expert fighters, but female lions are better hunters. Female lions are also strong, but they are built more for **stealth**. With their flexible bodies and finely tuned reflexes, they possess the grace of skilled predators.

Ancestors

Approximately 1.5 million years ago, animals similar to lions and tigers roamed an area of East Africa that is now called Olduvai Gorge. They are considered to be the first true ancestors of modern lions.

About 500,000 years ago, lions more like those living today appeared. These early lions were larger and more powerful than their modern counterparts. They also seem to have been great wanderers. Scientists have found fossils of their bones in China, Europe, and North America. About 10,000 years ago, the last traces of these feared creatures vanished.

Modern lions developed from those of the past alongside our own human ancestors. In fact, Olduvai Gorge has been a great source of fossil evidence for the study of early humans.

Did we hunt lions in the past, as we have in more recent times? Did they hunt us? We may never be certain. However, we do know this: artwork dating back tens of thousands of years indicates that our human relatives were as fascinated with their lions as we are with ours today.

UGANDA
KENYA
RWANDA
Lake Victoria
Olduvai Gorge
BURUNDI
DEMOCRATIC REPUBLIC OF THE CONGO
Lake Tanganyika
Indian Ocean
TANZANIA
0   200   400 km
0   200
MALAWI
Lake Nyasa
ZAMBIA
N
MOZAMBIQUE

LIFE SPAN

In captivity, where their existence is fairly safe and sheltered, lions can live as long as 25 or 30 years. In the wild, typical life spans are much shorter. Females live 16 to 18 years. Few males survive beyond the age of 12. An estimated three-quarters of males die violent deaths. Most are killed by humans or other lions.

Classification

Only one kind, or species, of lion is alive in the world today. Its scientific name is *Panthera leo*. The *Panthera* part of this name means that lions belong to the same family of cats as tigers, leopards, and jaguars. The *leo* part of the name refers to the species lion.

Two distinct types, or subspecies, of lions from two different continents exist today, the African lion and the Asiatic lion. Biologists distinguish between these two types of lions by adding another word to their scientific names. The African lion is called *Panthera leo leo*. The Asiatic lion is called *Panthera leo persica*.

Other subspecies of lions have existed in the past, but they are now extinct. Some of these extinctions occurred long ago. For example, the North American lion and the European cave lion died out at least 10,000 years ago. More recently, the black-maned Cape lion of southern Africa became extinct in 1865. The Barbary lion, once common throughout northern Africa, was wiped out in the early twentieth century. Neither subspecies could compete with the human need for farmland.

The lion that was used as a mascot for the Metro-Goldwyn-Mayer film studio was a Barbary lion. This type of lion is now extinct.

Can You Tell the Difference?

Although the African and Asiatic lions are similar, they have certain features that are distinctly different. Look at the pictures below, and read the points about each subspecies. What differences do you find?

Asiatic Lion

- The male's mane is usually short enough that his ears are almost always fully visible.
- Adult males typically weigh 350 to 420 pounds (160 to 190 kg). Females weigh 240 to 260 pounds (110 to 118 kg).
- The record length for a male, from nose to tail, is 9.5 feet (2.9 m). Most Asiatic lions are not this long.
- Asiatic lions have a long fold of skin that runs along the length of their bellies.
- The life span of Asiatic lions in the wild is 16 to 18 years.

African Lion

- An average adult male is about 9 feet (2.7 m) long from his nose to his tail. He stands 4 feet (1.2 m) at the shoulder.

- The average female is about 3.5 feet (1.1 m) tall at the shoulder and measures about 8 feet (2.4 m) in length.

- Adult females weigh from 265 to 400 pounds (120 to 182 kg). Males weigh from 330 to 550 pounds (150 to 250 kg).

- Males as heavy as 600 pounds (272 kg) and more have been observed but are rare in the wild.

Fur

Lions have short fur that ranges in color from pale sandy-tan to rich yellow-gold to dark chocolate-brown. The hair lining the belly and other underparts is usually white or near-white. The back of the ears and the furry tuft at the end of the tail are black.

While adults tend to lack the bold markings that decorate the fur of most other cats, cubs are speckled with spots on their legs, bellies, and foreheads. The spots usually disappear by adulthood, but some lions—especially those of East Africa—have faint spots throughout their lives.

The lion's most famous feature is the male's majestic, shaggy mane. This feature, unique among members of the cat family, frames the face and grows backward and downward to cover the neck, shoulders, and chest. A mane's color can vary from yellow to brown to black, and it is usually a mixture of these colors. A male's mane grows thicker and darker throughout its life.

The color of lion fur varies. While some lions have light yellow fur, the fur of other lions may be dark brown.

Special Adaptations

Lions have many **adaptations** or features that help them survive and thrive in their environment.

Eyes

With their large, golden-amber eyes, lions see about as well as humans during the day. At night, however, their pupils can open very wide—about three times bigger than the pupils of human eyes. This lets them collect light even when it is dark. Like all cats, lions have a light-reflecting surface on the back of their eyes to gather even more light. This surface causes the same glow you may have seen from a house cat's eyes. The more light their eyes gather, the better lions can see and hunt in the dark.

Lions are also experts at judging distances. This ability gives them a great advantage when stalking, chasing, and pouncing on prey.

Hearing

Much more is known about the hearing of house cats than about their wild relatives, the lions. Although some wildlife biologists believe that lions have better hearing than we do, there is little evidence to support their claims.

Lions can swivel their ears like radar receivers. This helps them detect and pinpoint sounds from any direction—another advantage when hunting.

A lion usually just "sees," or notices, things that are moving. If something is still, a lion does not see it.

When a lion is trying to hear something, its ears stand up straight.

Mouth

Lions have powerful jaws lined with thirty teeth. Two pairs of long, sharply pointed canine teeth at the front are used to hold on to and kill prey. The back teeth, called **carnassials**, are narrow and sharp. They work like scissors to slice flesh.

Lions do not have teeth for chewing, so they swallow their food in chunks. Rough, hook-like structures on the tongue work like sandpaper to help lions strip bits of meat from bones.

Paws

Soft pads on the bottoms of their paws help cushion and muffle each step as lions stalk their prey. Razor-sharp, curved claws help lions bring down prey and prevent it from escaping.

Lions have four claws on the back paws and five on the front. The fifth claw is a bit like a thumb that gives additional support for climbing or holding on to prey. Like

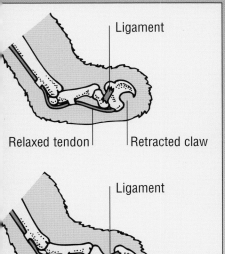

A cat's claws stay sharp partly because the cat keeps them retracted until it needs them.

Lions sometimes bare their teeth to keep other animals away from their food.

all cats, lions have **retractable claws** that are kept pulled in unless they are needed.

Mane

The male's most noticeable feature helps him in many ways. The mane acts like a thick, woolly scarf to protect his neck from the teeth or claws of unfriendly lions. It also emphasizes his size and strength. This can help him to frighten or intimidate other males, and make him look more attractive to females.

Mane color and size may help lions tell one male from another. This is especially important when lions approach one another from a distance.

The Pride

The pride is a family group made up of adult females, their cubs, and one or more adult males.

Opposite: Lions are the most social members of the cat family. They live in groups called prides.

Female lions make up the majority of a pride.

When it comes to family life, lions are more like wolves than other cats. Unlike most other cats, lions live and hunt in groups.

The most important unit of lion society is the pride. The pride is a family group made up of adult females, their cubs, and one or more adult males. All the females in a pride are related to one another—mothers, daughters, sisters, aunts, grandmothers, and cousins. The adult males are often, but not always, related to one another. They are never related to the females. The pride members live in the same area, play together, hunt together, and raise their families together. Outside of the pride, solitary **nomads** and groups of nomadic males form other social units.

Composition

Prides vary greatly in size. They can have as few as four lions or as many as forty. The average size of a pride is about fifteen.

Female lions are the focus of the pride. They inherit the pride territory from their relatives and usually stay there for their entire lives. Females raise the cubs, do most of the hunting, and help defend the pride and its land. Outsider females from other prides are especially unwelcome.

Adult males are temporary pride members. They may be part of the pride for only a few months or as long as several years. When males leave, it is usually because they have been driven out by other males who want to join the pride and mate with the females.

The males are responsible for keeping the pride—especially its cubs—safe from outsider lions as well as from other predators. They regularly mark and patrol the pride territory. They will defend their pride vigorously—to the death, if necessary.

Male members of a pride are immigrants who have won the right to mate with the females and be part of the pride.

Territory

Each pride lives in a home area, or territory, that has all the water and food its members need to survive. Some pride territories are fairly small, covering only about 15 square miles (39 sq km). Others can be ten times as large, covering 150 square miles (390 sq km).

The boundaries of the territory are not precisely defined. In most cases, territories overlap one another. Fortunately, confrontations, or battles between neighboring prides, do not happen very often.

Larger prides usually occupy larger territories. However, there are no firm rules. More than anything else, the amount of available food determines the size of the territory.

Male lions spend much of their time patrolling the boundaries of their territory.

Communication

Even though prides are close-knit groups, the members spend much of the time apart from one another. They often split into smaller groups to hunt, nurse cubs, or be with members of the same age or sex.

Pride lions may not see one another for weeks at a time, so it is important for them to be able to communicate their thoughts, feelings, and intentions to one another. Lions have many actions, body postures, odors, and sounds for expressing themselves.

Proclaiming Territory

Lions understand a great deal about one another through smell. They spray their strong-smelling urine on rocks, trees, bushes, and other plants throughout their territory. This lets pride members know when they are on safe ground. It also serves as a warning to outsider lions that they are near, or have entered, "private property." The males, as pride patrollers and defenders, do most of the spraying.

Lions also scrape their back feet on the ground, often urinating at the same time. This leaves a smelly and visible marking. Another method of marking territory is tree-raking. Lions have scent glands between their toes, so rubbing their paws along tree trunks leaves scratches and smells in the bark.

Roaring is another method lions use to communicate with pride members and outsiders. Roars can be heard from great distances—as far away as 5 miles (8 km) when the air is calm.

Because pride members are often separated, the roar can be an invitation to keep in touch. To pride members, it could translate as, "I am here. Where are you?" To outsider lions the roar is a warning that means, "This land is occupied. It is mine!"

Lions roar to communicate with other lions.

Signaling Friendly Intentions

When lions have not seen one another for a while, even if they have just been asleep, they often greet each other enthusiastically. You may have seen this behavior in house cats. It involves rubbing their heads and cheeks together. Cats, including lions, have a chin gland that releases their odor. Rubbing probably helps reduce aggression by distributing familiar smells. Sometimes lions rub their whole bodies against one another. This friendly rubbing behavior happens so often among pride members that it is called a greeting ceremony.

Another gesture lions use to show friendliness is licking. Like house cats, lions like to lick and groom one another—especially cubs and their mothers. They may also make a contented humming sound, which is the lion's version of a house cat's purr.

Showing Off for the Opposite Sex

When a female is ready to mate, she often trots in circles around the male, stroking him with her face, body, and tail. For a while, she may turn down his advances with a swipe of the paw or a playful skip away.

Males show off for females when they strut proudly in front of them. Strutting makes a male look bigger and more impressive. His head is held high, his mane is fully exposed, and his tail is arched broadly over his back.

Just like house cats, lions lick and groom one another.

More Communication

Expressing Anger or Fear

If you ever see an angry lion or one that is prepared to attack, you will know it. The head lowers, and the ears twist around to expose the black fur on the back. The eyes become large and stare ahead without blinking. The lion's weight is forward, its body tensed for immediate action. Growls and brief coughs accompany these actions and body positions. If the lion's tail is whipping up and down, attack is moments away.

Fearful or defensive lions crouch low to the ground, with their bodies leaning away from their opponent. Their ears are pasted flat against the side of their heads, and they snarl or hiss. They may roll over onto their sides or backs to indicate that they are not a threat, but they will fight if absolutely necessary. Usually the other lion respects this action and walks away.

Lions growl at other animals to keep them away from their kill.

Nomads

It is the destiny of all males to spend part, or sometimes all, of their lives as nomads—lions without a pride or home territory. Depending on where they live, adolescent males are forced out of their prides sometime between the ages of 18 months and 4 years.

Since all the best land already belongs to established prides, nomads usually do not have territories of their own. All these homeless lions exist on the edges of established pride territories or well beyond them. Some nomads wander over an area as large as 1,000 to 1,800 square miles (2,600 to 4,700 sq km).

Although some nomads spend their entire lives alone, most form **coalitions** with other nomads. The partners are often brothers or cousins from the same pride. However, coalitions between unrelated lions are also common.

Coalitions provide safety and companionship for their partners. They also serve another purpose. Groups of strong, healthy males are better able to challenge and fight males in existing prides. The coalition males then become the new pride males until they themselves are evicted by a stronger coalition.

Nomadic lions are sometimes those that have been defeated in a fight.

Lion Cubs

Almost helpless at birth, lion cubs rely on adult lions for food until they are at least 16 months old.

Opposite: A cub's eye color changes from cloudy blue to amber after a few months.

To most people, lion cubs are adorable. Their milky-blue, slightly crossed eyes, fluffy, spotted coats, wobbly bodies, tiny meows, and playful spirits make lion cubs hard to resist.

Almost helpless at birth, lion cubs rely on adult lions for food until they are at least 16 months old. Relying on adults carries a high price. Depending on where they live, 14 to 73 percent of all cubs are killed by predators or die from starvation or being abandoned within their first year of life.

A female lion must hide her cubs from hyenas, leopards, and other predators to keep them safe.

Mating

Lions do not have a specific mating season, so mating can happen during any month of the year. Several pride females usually go into **heat** at the same time. This sometimes occurs when a new male joins the pride. New males will kill the previous males' cubs so that the females will be ready to mate and have new cubs. Ordinarily, female lions will not be ready to mate until their cubs are grown and independent. This insures that the females will not have more cubs than they are able to raise.

During the four to six days that the females are in heat, males mate with them almost constantly—two or three times every hour. The males rarely get into squabbles over females.

It takes 100 to 120 days before a female gives birth to her litter. Shortly before that time, she withdraws from the pride to find a den. The den site she chooses is often the place where her mother gave birth to her. Most dens are in a sheltered, private area in dense vegetation or a rock outcropping.

During mating season, male lions stay with their partners and follow them wherever they go.

Newborns

Newborn cubs weigh 2 to 4.5 pounds (1 to 2 kg). They are totally defenseless and dependent on their mother, who stays with them for the first several weeks. She only leaves to hunt and eat with her pride.

While their mother is away, the cubs stay hidden in the den. This is the time when they are the most open to attack. Predators, such as leopards and hyenas, and even other lions, may sniff them out and eat them. Their mother sometimes moves them to a new den to avoid danger.

In four to six weeks, the cubs are old enough to walk and run around on their own. Then they are ready to meet other members of their pride.

A mother carries her cubs in her mouth for the first few weeks of their lives.

Care

Mothers and their cubs often live in a nursery-like grouping called a **crèche**. The cubs nurse, play, and develop as part of this group. Sometimes they meet, greet, and play with visitors from their pride. The crèche stays together until the cubs are old enough to look after themselves. This is not until they are about 18 months old.

Crèche cubs tend to be close to one another in age. If the difference in ages is too great—more than three months—the mother may choose to raise her cubs alone, away from her pride.

Even though mothers prefer to nurse and groom their own young, they do share their milk with other cubs. Roughly one-third of their milk feeds other cubs in the crèche. They will also look after another female's cubs if she dies.

Of the 37 different species of cats, lions and **feral** cats are the only ones that raise their young in a crèche.

A mother's milk provides all the nutrients young cubs need.

Identifying Individual Lions

Lions—especially the females—can look very similar. How do wildlife biologists tell them apart? The clues are primarily in the face. Many of these clues develop or are present when the lion is still a cub. Read the information below. Then see if you can tell the difference between the two lions at the bottom of the page.

- *Teeth:* Some teeth may be discolored, chipped, or missing.

- *Ears:* Sharp claws can cut slivers or chunks out of ears during play or fights over food.

- *Scars:* Scrapes and cuts often mark the nose, as well as other parts of the body. These can heal and fade over time, however.

- *Whiskers:* The whisker-spots on a lion's face are like a fingerprint. Each lion is born with its own distinctive whisker-spot pattern. It is visible throughout the lion's entire life and is the most reliable clue for telling lions apart.

Can you find some differences between these two lions?

Development

Birth – 2 Months

Cubs are usually born with their blue eyes shut. They open within three to fifteen days. It takes about another two to three more months before their eyes change to their permanent amber color.

Cubs crawl after their first day, but they do not walk well until they are about 3 weeks old. By this time, their first teeth have appeared, followed a week later by their first set of prey-killing, canine teeth. While meat-eating is now possible, cubs rarely get their first taste of meat until they are able to follow their mother to kills at about 2 months old. Even then, milk continues to be their main source of food.

2 Months – 1 Year

As the cubs near their third month, the spot-covered, fluffy, gray-yellow fur they were born with begins to take on a more adult color and appearance. Some males show the sparse beginnings of a mane by 6 months.

Cubs love to play. They box, wrestle, stalk, and pounce on one another, in addition to any adult or older relative who will put up with it. Adult females often play with cubs, usually chasing or lightly boxing with them.

Play helps cubs develop the skills and methods they will need to hunt. At around 11 months, cubs begin to learn about, and take part in, hunting.

Most lion litters contain two to four cubs.

1 – 2 Years

By the time they are 15 months old, most cubs weigh about 100 pounds (45 kg). In nine more months, they will have doubled their weight.

At about 15 to 16 months, cubs can catch and kill small prey on their own. Adult help is needed for larger prey until about the age of 2. Mothers stop looking after their cubs by the time they are 2 years old or, often, earlier. By this time, most females have new litters to raise.

2 – 4 Years

Adolescent males experience a growth spurt between the ages of 3 and 4. At age 4, they are nearly their adult weight and size. Some already have rich, full manes, while others are still developing theirs.

Females also grow during this period. Most have also developed into capable hunters. They are able to have cubs by age 2, but most do not mate until they are at least 4.

By age 6, males and females are their full adult size and weight.

Male lion cubs develop manes when they are 2 to 3 years old.

Habitat

*Opposite: Most lions live on the grasslands of Africa, known as the **savanna**.*

Lions survive in a wide range of habitats, but most live in grassland environments and open forest areas. Habitats such as the Serengeti Plains in East Africa and South Africa's Kruger National Park usually provide reliable water sources, plenty of food, and suitable cover for stalking prey.

Small numbers of lions make their homes in semidesert conditions, such as on the fringes of the Kalahari Desert. Some have been spotted as high as 13,900 feet (4,200 m) in the mountains of Ethiopia. Only thick, dense forests and dry, dusty deserts are unlikely homes for lions.

Lions share their environment with many other species of animals.

Daily Activities

When it comes to resting, lions are world champions. They spend 18 to 20 hours every day relaxing and sleeping. Their remaining time is largely devoted to hunting and feeding, most often under the cover of darkness.

When they are awake, lions are usually on the move. They frequently groom and play with other lions—activities that help strengthen family bonds. They may also patrol, and if necessary defend, the pride territory. Most of the time, males and females defend their territory against unwelcome lions of the same sex.

Because they spend so much time sleeping, lions are often thought of as being lazy. However, their long rests help them conserve the energy they need for an activity that is necessary for their survival: the search for food.

Lions usually rest for 18 to 20 hours a day.

Wildlife Biologists Talk About Lions

Judith Rudnai

"My association with Nairobi's lions lasted many happy years… witnessing mothers, daughters, and granddaughters return to the same area to give birth to yet another generation of Nairobi lions.… Hopefully, that will remain true for many future generations."

Judith Rudnai is a zoologist who has conducted important research on Nairobi's small population of lions and has written several books and articles about lions for both younger and older readers.

George Schaller

"At no time is [the movement of a lion] more vitally beautiful than when a lion tautly snakes toward its prey…a drama in which it was impossible not to participate emotionally, knowing that the death of a being hung in the balance."

George Schaller is an award-winning researcher who has made important contributions to the understanding of lions, gorillas, tigers, and a host of other animals.

Craig Packer

"[Well-studied lions] are interesting to us precisely because we know so much about their background.… Someone has to record all those tiny whisker spots for each cub, measure the size of each pride's territory, follow the fate of each frightened [juvenile] separated from its mother for the first time."

Craig Packer is a biology professor who has studied East Africa's lions closely since 1978. He and his wife, Anne Pusey, have proposed new theories about the origins of the social activities of lions.

Food

Lions lack the swiftness that graces most of their prey.

Opposite: Zebras are usually large enough to feed an entire pride. This makes them a favorite prey among lions.

These lions are chewing on a wildebeest, another favorite prey of lions.

Lions, like all cats, are carnivores, or meat-eaters. On a daily basis, they need about 11 pounds (5 kg) of meat to survive. When prey is plentiful and the hunt successful, lions may gorge on far more meat than they need, 70 pounds (32 kg) or more.

Lions are not particularly fast animals. With a top running speed of 35 miles (56 km) per hour, they lack the swiftness that graces most of their favorite prey. Instead, stealth, surprise, patience, and occasionally luck are their greatest assets when it comes to hunting.

What Lions Eat

Grassland and woodland lions generally prefer to prey upon medium-sized hoofed animals such as zebras, wildebeests, topis, and hartebeests.

However, lions are confident feeders that take advantage of an opportunity. They will eat whatever they can find, kill, or steal from other animals. Their prey includes smaller animals, such as impalas, porcupines, and warthogs, in addition to larger animals, such as buffaloes and giraffes.

During harsh times, when food supplies are more limited, lions will even make a meal out of insects, birds, fish, snakes, and—if they can crack them—ostrich eggs.

Impala
Warthog
Giraffe
Zebra
Snake
Wildebeest

Lions as Scavengers

Hunting takes a lot of time. It requires a great deal of energy, and success is never guaranteed. More prey escape a lion's clutches than are captured. This means lions are more than willing to take over another predator's catch. Given the chance, they **scavenge** kills from cheetahs, leopards, hyenas, and even other lions. Scavenging can account for up to half of a lion's total food intake! Lions also dine on animals they find dead from disease, old age, or injury.

Isolated in the heart of an extinct volcano that collapsed about two million years ago, the lions of Ngorongoro Crater in Tanzania are the lords of their land. With food almost always available, they have less need to hunt for themselves. As a result, they often scavenge kills from other predators.

How They Hunt

Stalking

If you have watched a house cat moving toward a mouse, bird, or toy, you have witnessed a version of one of the lion's most common hunting methods, stalking. Crouched low to the ground, back straight, eyes and ears fully tuned to its intended victim, moving slowly and quietly, the lion edges close enough to pounce on or rush at its prey.

The whole process may take half an hour or more, but it does not always result in capture. Stalking by herself, a female lion has only about a 17 percent chance of catching dinner. For a solitary male lion, the chances are even less.

Working Together

The odds of capturing prey become much better for lions if they hunt in groups. **Communal hunting** is mainly the job of female lions. Sometimes they surround the intended prey from all sides and close in. Another technique involves one or several lions lying in wait as other lions drive prey toward them.

No other cats use such deliberate cooperation to capture prey. Bringing down an adult African buffalo weighing nearly 1 ton (900 kg) would be impossible without the coordinated efforts of several lions working toward a common goal.

Lions usually circle their prey from a distance before they go in for the kill.

This lion is chasing a hyena.

The Kill

Lions usually kill large prey by biting at its neck or mouth. Biting at the neck crushes the windpipe, and the animal is strangled. Biting over the mouth prevents the animal from breathing, and it suffocates. Neither method is quick. Death may take as long as 13 minutes. However, prey show little sign of struggle. Most are probably in a state of shock. Small prey can be swatted to the ground, and a bite to any part of their head or body will kill them.

The Feed

Cooperation seems to break down when it is time to eat. Even though males rarely take part in the hunt, they usually get to eat first. On some occasions, especially if many lions are present and if they are very hungry, the scene turns into an angry, snarling frenzy.

Sometimes the males will allow cubs to feast alongside them. Otherwise, cubs are forced to dart in and out of the lion-covered carcass, scrounging whatever tidbits they can.

A mother will usually eat before her cubs. Some females steal food from cubs. Not surprisingly, many cubs die from starvation.

Competition

At kills, conflicts can be intense between lions fighting for a fair share.

Within the pride, competition usually centers around food. Cubs fight aggressively for milk. Smaller cubs are frequently pushed aside by larger cubs unless the female is involved. At kills, conflicts can be intense between lions fighting for a fair share. Torn, bloody ears are common as hungry adults, adolescents, and cubs wrestle and box one another for a spot to feed from.

Opposite: Visual displays of anger are sometimes enough to drive off a competitor.

Angry lions hiss and snarl at one another.

Competing with Other Lions

Lions are **territorial**. They defend their area or territory. Lionesses usually chase off unfamiliar females that stray too far into the pride's territory. Males guard the pride against intruding males. However, lions generally avoid direct confrontations whenever possible.

The main exception to this occurs during a pride takeover. The battle between the pride males and the challenging males is usually brutal. Males on either side often suffer serious injury or death.

Competing with Other Predators

Lions are the largest, most powerful predators in their environment. They often steal from and sometimes kill their cat relatives, the cheetah and the leopard. The only predator capable of standing up to the lion is the hyena.

Hyenas and lions share a taste for many of the same kinds of prey. Not surprisingly, conflicts between these two predators are common. Each readily scavenges food from the other. Each will also pester or attack the other. Hyenas are reluctant to take on male lions. However, a large mob of loud, aggressive hyenas can send a small group of adult females fleeing in snarling terror. Lions rarely eat the hyenas they kill, but hyenas will feast on lion meat if they have the chance.

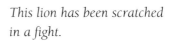

This lion has been scratched in a fight.

Competing with Humans

Another animal species is even more territorial than lions—humans. People often carefully guard the land they have, and some people's desire for more land continues to grow.

With each new farm, industrial complex, and settlement, conflicts between people and lions become inevitable. When lions get too close, or threaten the safety of cattle and other livestock, they are often shot.

A much smaller threat to lions comes from hunting. Although ten African countries prohibit lion-hunting, several provide no such protection. Hunting for sport is still allowed in six African countries, and fourteen others allow hunting of lions that are considered to be dangerous or to pose a problem.

In the Ngorongoro Crater in Tanzania, the Masai people, their cattle, and the lions share land with little conflict.

Lions are often used in heraldry, a system of symbols used to represent a person, family, or institution. A set of symbols is also called a coat of arms or a crest. Lions are popular symbols, often meaning courage.

Folklore

In the lion, many cultures have long recognized the values and qualities they cherish most: nobility, majesty, courage, and— above all—power. Therefore, it was natural for people to use lions as symbols of royalty. Legend has it that the Egyptian Pharaoh, Ramses II, rode into battle with a lion by his side. Royal families of Great Britain and Europe decorated their family crests and coats of arms with lions. An African chief would carry a staff bearing a lion carving as a symbol of his authority.

Even in North America, where wild lions became extinct over 10,000 years ago, people still idolize the animal's power and prestige.

Lions commonly appear on products as varied as T-shirts, business logos, cars, and sports uniforms. Some lions sit as stone guardians in front of public buildings such as libraries and city halls.

This lion guards the city as it sits on top of a bridge.

45

Folklore History

People express their admiration of lions through art, literature, religion, myth, and legend. Over 30,000 years ago in Germany, an ivory lion mask was made for the face of a human figurine. About 15,000 years later, an unknown painter captured the image of a lion on a cave wall in France.

Lions were worshiped as gods in the ancient Middle East, Africa, and India. They still play a role in the rituals and traditions of many peoples from these lands. In China, the Lion Dance is performed at New Year celebrations to bring joy and good fortune.

Lions often appear as monstrous "combination creatures" in the lore of different cultures. For instance, the sphinx of Greek and Egyptian mythology had a lion's body and a human head. In India, the mythical Yali combined the body of a lion with the face of an elephant. The European Manticore mixed the lion's body with a human head and a scorpion's or dragon's tail.

In Greek mythology, a sphinx had a woman's head, a lion's body, two wings, and a serpent's tail.

Myths vs. Facts

Lions cannot climb trees.

Lions can and do climb trees—sometimes as high as 23 feet (7 m) off the ground. Lions climb trees to play, find a private resting spot, and escape from danger.

Female lions are bad mothers.

Most females are intensely protective mothers. This myth comes from the fact that some females abandon their litters, especially if there is only a single cub. Biologists believe that in such cases, the female's bond with her pride may be stronger than her mothering instincts. Leaving a single cub means the female will be able to mate again soon, perhaps producing a larger litter. Nobody knows for sure if these reasons are true.

Lions hunt people for food.

Lions rarely kill and eat people. Most of the small number of lions who begin eating people do so because these lions are old, disabled, or starving. This was the case from the early 1930s to 1947 when a pride of 15 lions killed an estimated 1,000 to 1,500 people in southern Tanzania.

Folktales

Lions are featured in the biblical stories of Samson and Daniel. They also appear in the myths and legends of many cultures. Sometimes the lions are fierce, sometimes they are godlike, sometimes they have big egos, and sometimes—especially in African folktales—they are outsmarted by smaller, more cunning animals.

Helpful Lions

In this Ethiopian tale, a wild lion helps a woman learn how to gain the love and respect of her new stepson.

Day, Nancy Raines. *The Lion's Whiskers: An Ethiopian Folktale.* New York: Scholastic, 1995.

Find out how a grateful lion helps a Greek slave in this version of a classic tale by the African/Greek storyteller, Aesop. Many editions of this story exist. Check your local library for other versions.

Nolan, Dennis, and Aesop. *Androcles and the Lion.* San Diego: Harcourt, 1997.

Odd Lions

In a very strange tale called "Leftovers," find out how Lion is made, how he becomes the King of Beasts, and why he needs to watch out for Wild Bull.

Hughes, Ted. *Tales of the Early World.* London: Faber, 1988.

Foolish Lions

Join in the quest as the lion and other African animals try to earn the fruit of a magic tree in this retelling of a Bantu story.

Lottridge, Celia Barker. *The Name of the Tree: A Bantu Tale.* New York: M.K. McElderry Books, 1987.

See the lion outsmarted by a rabbit in "Lion Outwitted by Hare" and by a bird in "The Lion and the Little Brown Bird" in these tales from the peoples of Africa.

Savory, Phyllis. *Lion Outwitted by Hare and other African Tales.* Chicago: Whitman, 1971.

Smile as a lion and stoat (weasel) compete with each other.

Zelinsky, Paul O. *The Lion and the Stoat.* New York: Greenwillow, 1984.

Magical Lions

Meet Aslan, the golden lion-god, as he enlists the help of four children who step through an enchanted wardrobe to the land of Narnia. If you like this adventure, check out the six other books in the Narnia series.

Lewis, C.S. *The Lion, the Witch, and the Wardrobe.* New York: HarperCollins, 1997.

Lions and other cats are explored through folktales, proverbs, and sayings in this collection of stories.

Leach, Maria. *The Lion Sneezed: Folktales and Myths of the Cat.* New York: Crowell, 1977.

Lion Distribution in Africa

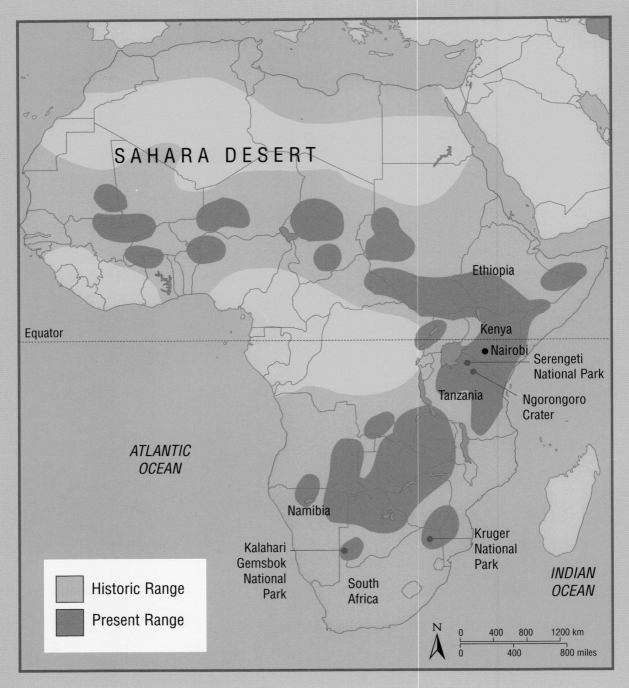

SAHARA DESERT

Ethiopia

Kenya

Equator

• Nairobi

Serengeti
National Park

Tanzania

Ngorongoro
Crater

ATLANTIC
OCEAN

Namibia

Kruger
National
Park

INDIAN
OCEAN

Kalahari
Gemsbok
National
Park

South
Africa

Historic Range

Present Range

N

| 0 | 400 | 800 | 1200 km |
| 0 | | 400 | 800 miles |

Status

Today, almost all lions live in Africa, south of the Sahara Desert.

The dark shaded areas on the map (left) indicate where lions live in Africa. They have disappeared from much of the continent. The lion in India is dangerously close to extinction.

Large populations of lions once roamed freely across Europe, the Middle East, southwest Asia, and much of Africa. Today, almost all lions live in Africa, south of the Sahara Desert. Estimates of their numbers range from 30,000 and to 100,000.

The only wild representatives of the once-widespread Asiatic lion are confined to the Gir Forest—a 545-square-mile (1,412 sq km) sanctuary in western India. Their numbers, about 100 at the start of the twentieth century, are now thought to be between 200 and 300.

Several factors have contributed to the lion's decline. However, two in particular have resulted in the highest casualties: hunting and loss of habitat.

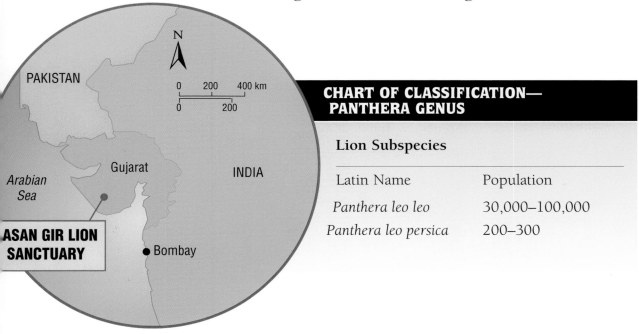

CHART OF CLASSIFICATION— PANTHERA GENUS

Lion Subspecies

Latin Name	Population
Panthera leo leo	30,000–100,000
Panthera leo persica	200–300

Decline in Population

Lion populations have declined for two main reasons: loss of habitat and hunting.

Habitat Loss

Africa has committed a significant portion of its land to preserving lions and other wildlife. More than 10 percent of East and southern Africa is now protected. Another 8 percent of southern Africa is wildlife land. However, this represents a mere fraction of the lion's former range.

The growing human population in Africa and India needs space to live and more farmland for growing food and raising livestock. There is little land left for creating new parks and nature preserves where lions can roam free and undisturbed.

Meanwhile, lions from existing parks sometimes wander outside or break through the boundary fences. Farmers, fearing for their families and livestock, often shoot trespassing lions. In 1996, for example, 14 of 21 starving lions that broke through the fence surrounding Kalahari Gemsbok National Park in South Africa were shot after they raided a farmer's sheep farm.

The territory of many lions has been made into parkland to protect the lions and halt development.

Hunting

Among Africa's native peoples, lion-hunting is a long-standing tradition. In East Africa, young Masai warriors once showed their courage and valor by hunting lions at spearpoint. Since relatively few lions were killed, this hunting had little impact on lion populations as a whole.

This situation changed dramatically during the early 1900s. Big-game hunters from all over the world massacred many lions for sport. The lions they killed were usually taken as trophies to mount on their walls back at home.

To the African governments that allow it, hunting is an important part of their tourist industry. Hunters pay as much as $30,000 for the right to kill lions. For poor nations, or those with limited financial resources, this money is hard to turn down. Increasingly, the money earned from safari hunting is paid directly to the rural communities that live with wildlife, such as lions, to fund local programs.

In Africa, reserves now exist to keep many lions safe from hunters. Hunters are still allowed to kill lions in certain areas, but they must have a special license.

Steep Decline in Population

Disease

In early 1994, distressing reports began to trickle out of Serengeti National Park in East Africa. The lions had been infected with a virus that caused convulsions, seizures, and painful death.

Researchers later identified the disease as a form of **canine distemper**. It had been passed on to the lions by hyenas that were in contact with pet dogs living outside the park. A campaign was launched to vaccinate the estimated 20,000 to 30,000 dogs. But the damage had been done. By the time the disease had run its course, 1,000 lions—one-third of the park's population—had died.

Diseases are a natural part of all environments, but this disease was different. It was directly related to the growing numbers of people—and their pets—around the park. Incidents like this have happened before in Africa. They are hard to predict and control.

Scientists learn more about lions by studying and helping those in zoos. This lion is having an operation on one of his teeth.

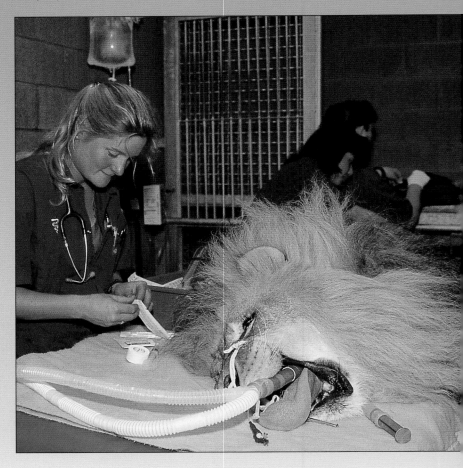

Inbreeding

Usually, the chances of **inbreeding** among lions are low because adolescent males are expelled from the pride before they can mate with their sisters and cousins. When populations of lions are isolated, the chances of inbreeding increase.

For example, about 100 lions currently make their home in Ngorongoro Crater in Tanzania. The steep crater walls have, for the most part, prevented most of the lions from leaving and all but a few new lions from getting in.

In 1962, an overpopulation of blood-sucking flies left lions with open wounds, which weakened them and

Lions in the Ngorongoro Crater can only breed amongst themselves.

eventually killed 60 of the 70 lions in the crater. Since this time, inbreeding has set in among the surviving lions. Most of the crater's current population of lions are closely related to one another. This makes them vulnerable to disease and birth defects because they are too similar at a **genetic** level. Genetic similarities have also been found among Asiatic lions, in the wild as well as in zoos.

Other lion populations across Africa are isolated because of human developments around parks and wilderness areas. So there is a chance that inbreeding could happen there, too.

55

Viewpoints

Should people be able to keep lions in private zoos?

A growing number of small zoos have sprung up throughout North America and Europe. These zoos are different from the large zoos found in most major cities around the world. Large zoos are like companies. They have managers, executives, specially trained staff, and boards of directors. Private zoos are usually owned by one or two people who live on the same property as the zoo.

PRO

1 Private zoos help people learn more about lions and the other animals in the zoo. Some people live too far away from large zoos.

2 Private zoos often give homes to lions that thoughtless people bought as pets. These animals would otherwise be abandoned, abused, or killed.

3 Some private zoos are involved in genetic research and captive breeding programs to help increase or reestablish wild populations of lions.

CON

1 Only a few private zoos run informative, accurate education programs. The rest tend to be more interested in profit than learning. In most cases, educational signs, if they are present at all, contain inaccurate or misleading information.

2 Some private zoos are animal sanctuaries for rescued lions and other mistreated animals. The majority, however, are poorly run. They provide inadequate and usually unhealthy living conditions for their animals.

3 Most private zoo owners know little or nothing about breeding programs. They also lack the scientific knowledge and experience to conduct the programs properly.

Protecting the Asiatic Lion

The Asiatic lion has been listed as an endangered species since the 1970s. Although the Gir Forest population is healthy, it is still very small.

In 1981, a Species Survival Plan (a program sponsored by the American Zoological Association) was laid out for the 200 or so Asiatic lions in North American and European zoos. The idea was to treat the zoo lions as a "captive population" spread out over two continents. This way, if anything happened to the Gir lions, members from the captive population could be reintroduced to the wild. Genetic testing later showed that only a few of the zoo animals were pure Asiatic lions. The rest were mixtures of Asiatic and African lions.

A similar plan is now underway among European zoos, without American involvement. By April 1997, there were 12 zoos involved in the European Breeding Program. At that time, there were 32 pure Asiatic lions in captivity.

In 1994, India agreed to establish a second wild population of its lions. The new habitat is the Palpur Kuno Wildlife Sanctuary, northwest of the Gir Forest. Thousands of people and cattle still live in the area, so many details still have to be worked out before this second wild population prowls around its new home.

Unlike that of the African lion, the Asiatic lion's mane does not cover its ears.

What You Can Do

You can start helping lions by learning as much as possible about them. Read books and watch nature documentaries. Write to one of the organizations below. Find out what they do so you can decide whether you would like to be a part of their activities. Most importantly, share what you learn so other people can be as well-informed about lions as you are.

Conservation Groups

INTERNATIONAL

World Conservation Union (IUCN)
Rue Mauverney 28
CH 1196 Gland
Switzerland

Born Free Foundation
UK Head Office
3 Grove House
Fandry Lane
Horsham, Sussex
RH13 5PL
United Kingdom

The Asiatic Lion Information Centre
5 Medway House
Samuel Street
Preston, Lancashire
PR1 4YJ
United Kingdom

UNITED STATES

World Wildlife Fund
1250 - 24th Street NW
Washington, DC
20037

Cat Tales Endangered Species Conservation Park
N. 17020 Newport Hwy
Mead, WA
99021

African Wildlife Foundation
1400 - 16th Street, NW
Suite 120
Washington, DC
20036

CANADA

World Wildlife Fund Canada
245 Eglinton Avenue E.
Suite 410
Toronto, Ontario
M4P 3J6

Zoocheck Canada
3266 Yonge Street
Suite 1729
Toronto, Ontario
M4N 3P6

African Lion Safari
RR #1
Cambridge, Ontario
N1R 5S2

Twenty Fascinating Facts

1 Lions are great opportunists when it comes to food. A pride living near the Skeleton Coast desert in Namibia learned how to hunt Cape seals. Unfortunately, cattle-herders killed all of the pride members in 1991.

2 A lion's claws can be as long as 3 inches (7.6 cm).

3 Lions can leap a distance of 30 feet (9 m).

4 The word "pride" to describe lion families first appeared in print in 1450. No one knows who invented it or when it was first used.

5 What do you get if you mate a lion with a tiger? If it is a male lion and a female tiger, the cub is called a "liger." When it is a male tiger and a female lion, the cub is a "tiglon."

6 Fossils in Alaska, the Yukon, Alberta, and California show that lions once lived in North America. These "American

7 Stone lions often stand guard at the entrance to Buddhist temples. To Buddhists, lions represent defenders of the law.

8 During the European Middle Ages, many people believed that lion cubs were born dead and stayed that way for three days. On the third day, their father brought them to life by breathing on them.

9 The manes of lions in captivity tend to grow longer and thicker than those of wild lions.

10 In Africa, many people believe that tribal chiefs and other important figures can be **reincarnated** as lions. Two East African lions who ate dozens of railroad builders in 1898 were believed to be an ancient king and queen who had returned from the dead.

11 For an unknown reason, many of the lions who live in Tanzania's Selous Game Reserve do not have manes.

12 Lions in the Kalahari Desert have learned how to deal with the shortage of water. They eat melons that contain a large amount of water.

13 Male Asiatic lions, unlike their African cousins, do not spend much time with the females of their pride. The males usually keep to themselves unless they are mating or the females have made a large kill.

14 Once in a while, white-furred lions are born in Timbavati, a part of South Africa's Kruger National Park. Because these rare lions have amber eyes, they are not true **albinos**.

15 Lions have the largest eyes of all the world's carnivorous animals.

16 Lions appear in the sacred writings and art of many of the world's major religions, including Buddhism, Christianity, Hinduism, and Judaism.

17 The kind of lion that roars at the start of all MGM movies does not exist in the wild anymore. The Barbary lion has been extinct since the 1920s.

18 Like all cats, lions make a sneering or grimacing face when they smell urine or other interesting scents. They have a smelling and tasting organ in the roof of their mouths. When they make the grimace face, they suck the smells into their mouths to be sensed by this special organ.

19 Moving lion cubs to a new den or to a crèche can involve traveling great distances. Three females in Tanzania moved their 12 cubs 5 miles (8 km) in one night!

20 Lions have very tough skin. The ancient Greeks may have used this fact in inventing the legendary Nemean lion. This lion had skin so hard it could not be penetrated by metal. When Hercules killed the lion, he wore its hide like a suit of armor.

Glossary

adaptations: Changes made to fit into a certain environment

albinos: Animals that have no coloring. Such animals usually have white fur and red eyes.

canine distemper: A deadly disease, caused by a virus, that usually infects dogs

carnassials: The sharp teeth at the very back of the mouth of meat-eating animals

coalition: Two or more male lions that join together in a temporary group

communal hunting: Hunting that is done by a group of female lions

crèche: A group of mothers and their cubs

feral: Having escaped domestication and become wild

genetic: Relating to genes, which determine the characteristics of all living things

heat: The period of time during which a female lion is ready and willing to mate with a male lion

inbreeding: When very closely related lions, such as brothers and sisters, mate and have cubs together

nomads: Male lions who have neither a pride nor territory of their own and wander through the areas outside of the pride territories

reincarnation: The belief that when a person or animal dies, it is reborn as another person or animal

retractable claws: Claws that can be pulled back into the paw when not in use

savanna: Grasslands

scavenge: When an animal eats dead animals that it has not killed

stealth: The act of moving quietly and undercover

territorial: Having a strong sense of ownership of an area

Suggested Reading

Adamson, Joy. *Born Free: A Lioness of Two Worlds*. New York: Random House, 1987.

Caras, Roger. *Mara Simba: The African Lion*. New York: Holt Rinehart & Winston, 1988.

Hanby, Jeannette. *Lions Share: The Story of a Serengeti Pride*. Boston: Houghton Mifflin, 1982.

Harman, Amanda. *Lions*. New York: Benchmark, 1997.

Moss, Cynthia. *Portraits in the Wild*. Chicago: University of Chicago Press, 1982.

Packer, Craig. *Into Africa*. Chicago: University of Chicago Press, 1994.

Schaller, George. *The Serengeti Lion*. Chicago: University of Chicago Press, 1972.

Schaller, George. *Wonders of Lions*. New York: Putnam, 1977.

LIONS ON THE INTERNET

One of the places you can find out more about lions is on the Internet. Visit the following sites, or try searching on your own:

Planet Lion
http://www.planet-pets.com/pIntlion.htm

The Kingdom of Lions
http://www.rlion.cistron.nl/lkindex.htm

African Lion Working Group
http://www.african-lion.org/lions.htm

The Lion Research Center – University of Minnesota
http://www.lionresearch.org

Index